DEFEND AND PROTECT

UNDERCOVER OPERATIONS

Sarah Levete

Gareth Stevens
PUBLISHING

Peachtree

Please visit our website, **www.garethstevens.com**.
For a free color catalog of all our high-quality books,
call toll free 1-800-542-2595 or fax 1-877-542-2596.

Cataloging-in-Publication Data

Levete, Sarah.
Undercover operations / by Sarah Levete.
p. cm. — (Defend and protect)
Includes index.
ISBN 978-1-4824-4127-7 (pbk.)
ISBN 978-1-4824-4128-4 (6-pack)
ISBN 978-1-4824-4129-1 (library binding)
1. Intelligence service — Juvenile literature.
2. Undercover operations — Juvenile literature.
3. Espionage — Juvenile literature. I. Levete, Sarah. II. Title.
JF1525.I6 L48 2016
327.12—d23

First Edition

Published in 2016 by
Gareth Stevens Publishing
111 East 14th Street, Suite 349
New York, NY 10003

© 2016 Gareth Stevens Publishing

Produced by Calcium
Editors: Sarah Eason and Jennifer Sanderson
Designers: Paul Myerscough and Simon Borrough
Picture research: Jennifer Sanderson

Picture credits: Department of Defense (DoD): 29, Staff Sgt. David Bennett 38b, 38c; Dreamstime:
American Spirit 7b, 11b, 17b, 23b, 31b, 39b, Bluraz 43, Charles Mccarthy 41, Intst 24, Mike2focus
35, Pixattitude 5c, 8b, 13t, 15b, 19b, 21b, 25b, 27b, 29b, 33b, 35b,36b, 41b, 43b, Wernerimages
10; Allyson Kitts 37, Art Konovalov 3, 18, David Stuart Productions 4, Everett Historical 30, Frederic
Legrand - COMEO 33, GlebStock 22, Karenfoleyphotography 6, Mark Van Scyoc 17, Mauro Grigollo
25, Phase4Studios 40, Prometheus72 7, Studio10Artur 8, Svetlana Lukienko 14, Wally Stemberger
32, wowstudio 19; US Navy: Mass Communication Specialist 3rd Class Travis K. Mendoza 1, 27,
Photographer's Mate 2nd Class Eric S. Logsdon 26; Wikimedia Commons: 31, 5, 45, Muhammad
ud-Deen 39, Dr Julius Neubronner 21, Marcus.rosentrater 34, Mary Anne Fackelman 42, Mike Mozart
20, Pete Souza, Official White House Photographer 13,
Staff Sgt. Tyrone Clakely 12.

Printed in the United States of America

CPSIA compliance information: Batch #CW16GS: For further information contact
Gareth Stevens, New York, New York at 1-800-542-2595.

Contents

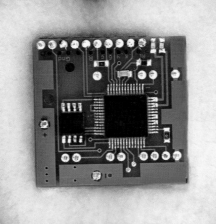

CHAPTER 1:
A World of Secrets

A deadly gun hidden in lipstick, secret messages in invisible ink, a cat fitted with a listening device: which of these were used in undercover operations? Read on and find out! Undercover operations feature some amazing gadgets, but there is more to undercover work than high-tech gizmos. Going undercover is risky and dangerous. Around the world, the armed forces, secret services, police, and other organizations send men and women on hazardous undercover missions.

Secret agent

Operations are often given a code name to add to their secrecy. Operation Paper clip involved the United States getting information from Nazi scientists (right) without the Nazis knowing.

The Undercover World

An undercover operation is an investigation carried out with utmost secrecy. Sometimes, undercover agents or operatives take on different identities, pretending to be someone else. People who apply for undercover operations need to be expert liars, great at keeping secrets, and prepared to risk their lives for their country. It takes a certain type of individual to make it as an undercover operative because the agent needs to be totally committed to the job.

This book takes you undercover to find out who works on secret missions and why. Read on to find out about the dangers of this secretive work.

THINK LIKE AN AGENT

Undercover agents often use invisible ink to send and receive secret messages. The KGB (secret service of the former Soviet Union) equipped some of its spies with lipstick guns—4.5 mm, single-shot weapons that could be carried inside a purse. The United States agency, the Central Intelligence Agency (CIA), fitted a cat with a listening device to eavesdrop on the KGB. However, the cat ran off into the path of a taxi and was killed before it revealed any secrets!

Why Undercover?

Undercover operations take place when there is no other way of getting information that will help expose a criminal network. It is used for some of the most serious crimes, when the only way to uncover the criminals and stop them is to infiltrate them. Spies work undercover for their country or another organization in order to uncover confidential and top-secret information. Organizations send their operatives undercover when they do not want others to know what they are doing.

The threat from global terrorism is spreading. Going undercover is often the only way that security services and intelligence agencies can remain one step ahead of the terrorists, and prevent terrorist atrocities. Sometimes, men and women are sent undercover in their own country to infiltrate groups that the security services consider a threat.

Fake passport

Too Secret?

Although secrecy is the key to success in undercover work, too much secrecy leads to concerns. If little is known about undercover operations, how does the public know that they are being carried out for a country's best interests? On the other hand, without secrecy, undercover operations would be compromised and the missions probably abandoned.

Undercover operations are often used to help find terrorists and prevent attacks, such as this one in Turkey in 2003.

THINK LIKE AN UNDERCOVER AGENT

An undercover agent infiltrating an extremist group has to pretend to share the extremists' beliefs. These beliefs go against the agent's own beliefs. The agent sometimes has to stand back and let the extremists continue to say and plan terrible things. The aim is for the agent to gather enough information to put a stop to the group's activity, by secretly passing on its plans to the security services and police who can stop the group.

TAKE THE TEST!

Do you have what it takes to go undercover?

ANSWERS

Undercover operatives need to be observant and able to remember tiny details. How much can you remember about what you have read?

Q1. Why do undercover agents use false IDs?

Q2. An agent is allowed to tell family and friends about undercover work as long as they trust them. True or false?

Q3. Why do some people have concerns about undercover work?

Q4. When agents are working undercover, they must stop any criminal activity. True or false?

Q5. Are undercover operations used for everyday crimes such as burglary?

Q6. Why did the CIA fit a cat with a listening device?

Q7. Why did the KGB give agents weapons hidden in lipstick cases?

Q8. Does an agent always agree with the aims of the group they are spying on?

Q8. No. Agents often go undercover with groups whose beliefs they completely disagree with

Q7. Because no one would be suspicious when someone took out a lipstick case from their purse

Q6. In order to listen to KGB conversations and discover KGB secrets

Q5. No. They are used when the only way to stop a criminal group is to infiltrate it

Q4. False. Sometimes an agent has to stand by and not say anything even when crimes are being committed

Q3. Because there is no way of knowing whether secretive undercover work is being carried out for a country's best interest

Q2. False. Agents must not reveal details of their undercover work, even to close family

Q1. So the operation is kept secret

CHAPTER 2:
Undercover in the United States

In the United States, armed forces' elite units, and government agencies such as the Federal Bureau of Investigation (FBI) and the CIA, sometimes work undercover. The nature of undercover work means that colleagues who work closely with someone undercover are completely unaware of their workmate's involvement. A web of secrecy is needed to keep the undercover operation safe from discovery.

People who work undercover do not let others know what they are doing. This protects their safety and makes sure the mission remains secret.

A Long Haul

It takes patience and time to build up the trust of those with whom agents are trying to work. Two operations, "Smoking Dragon" and "Royal Charm," uncovered a huge criminal network that smuggled illegal drugs, weapons, and counterfeit money. The operations began as an investigation into the trade of illegal cigarettes. The undercover agents soon realized that the network was involved in other dangerous activities. The network was smuggling deadly weapons and illegal drugs.

Working alongside other agencies, including the United States Secret Service, FBI agents posed as drug traffickers, arms traffickers, and other underworld criminals. In order to arrest some of the suspects who were based overseas, the FBI sent out invitations to a fake wedding on a yacht. The criminals arrived for the wedding, only to be arrested.

THINK LIKE A DEEP UNDERCOVER AGENT

An agent who goes undercover needs a cover story and an alias—they pretend to be someone else. Criminals will be suspicious of new acquaintances and will be on the lookout for people trying to trick them. Many agents use their own name as their alias. Agents might be unlucky and meet someone from their real life while undercover. If they are greeted by their own name, it will make their cover more believable.

Undercover with the CIA

The CIA collects information from foreign sources that will help defend and protect the United States. The president of the United States gives authorization for the CIA to undertake covert missions.

Black Hawk

Surveillance

Osama bin Laden was the world's most wanted terrorist. He was held responsible for coordinating the attacks on the United States' World Trade Center and the Pentagon in September 2001. Some 10 years after bin Laden became a hunted man, the CIA thought it was onto him. A large and well-concealed compound in a wealthy part of Pakistan was attracting the interest of agents on the ground, but the compound's high walls and privacy screens prevented anyone from seeing inside. All trash was burned inside the compound. This activity began to raise suspicion.

The CIA set up surveillance. Undercover, operatives asked casual questions about the families who lived in the compound. They pretended they wanted to buy property in the area. The snippets of information they gleaned, telephone conversations the CIA listened into, and secret satellite imagery of the compound, led CIA analysts to believe that the compound was indeed home to bin Laden.

ACT LIKE A CIA UNDERCOVER AGENT

A crucial mission can easily go dangerously wrong. If agents raise suspicion by asking too many questions or by seeming out of place, missions are compromised. Even when agents think they have come across a key piece of information, patience and calm are crucial. Panic will betray the mission and risk lives.

After months of preparation, President Obama gave the green light for the mission to capture bin Laden. In the dead of night, Night Stalkers (the United States' Special Forces unit) flew their Black Hawk helicopters over the area. Special Forces SEALs stealthily emerged from the helicopters to storm the compound. The mission to find bin Laden was underway.

President Barack Obama and his closest team watch a live feed of the attack on what was believed to be bin Laden's hideout.

13

Undercover with the FBI

Before employing an agent, the FBI will ask family, friends, and neighbors about the applicant, to make sure it employs the right people. On some undercover operations, the FBI recruits people from inside an organization or suspected criminal network to work for the Bureau. These people are known as informers. The FBI agent who manages the informer is known as the handler.

The Mafia and other criminal networks make huge amounts of money from their criminal activities. Going undercover is dangerous but often the only way the police can gather evidence about such criminal networks.

Donnie the Jeweler

In 1976, FBI agent Joe Pistone took the name Donnie Brasco, and created a legend (a false identity and history) for himself as a jewel thief. He went undercover to find out about crimes that the FBI believed were linked to the Mafia. To make his legend believable, Pistone studied street values of all precious gems and learned how to pick locks and disable alarms. "Donnie" went to New York City and became known to some of the Mafia as a jewel thief.

For six years, the Mafia accepted Donnie Brasco. When they asked him to kill someone, Pistone knew that his cover would be blown if he refused. The FBI decided to pull him out. However, Pistone had already gathered enough evidence to convict 100 members of the Mafia. It was an incredibly dangerous mission. Only a few in the FBI were aware of the operation. Donnie risked recognition by someone who knew him as Pistone. His recording devices could have been discovered, too. Joe Pistone and his family still live under assumed names and there is a contract for Joe's death hanging over his head.

ACT LIKE A DEEP UNDERCOVER AGENT

Undercover agents like Pistone have to sacrifice their family life. Working deep undercover means agents see their family only a few times a month. The agents are unable to share any details of their double lives. They cannot share work problems with those closest to them.

TAKE THE TEST!

Could you be an undercover team player?

Answer these questions to see if you could be a handler or part of an undercover team:

Q1. What does FBI stand for?

Q2. What are the Night Stalkers?

Q3. Why do some agents use their real first name as their alias?

Q4. What is a handler?

Q5. Why was Joe Pistone pulled out of his undercover operation?

Q6. Why do you think Pistone still lives under a false name?

Q7. What clues did the CIA have that Osama bin Laden was hiding in a compound in Pakistan?

Q8. Why do you think the FBI finds out about people's lives before employing them?

ANSWERS

Q1. Federal Bureau of Investigation

Q2. A US Special Forces unit

Q3. Because it helps them maintain their role if they meet someone who calls them by their real name

Q4. The FBI agent who manages the informer or agent

Q5. He was being asked to kill someone. Refusing to do so would have blown his cover

Q6. Because he betrayed criminals who might want to seek revenge

Q7. The compound was completely shielded from outside view, and all trash was burned inside

Q8. To make sure it employs that right people

CHAPTER 3:
Eyes and Ears

Undercover operations rely on agents and informers gathering intelligence, or intel. Their jobs are made much easier by high-tech devices. Once they have the intel, agents need to get it back to their handlers or bosses without blowing their cover. From listening tools to invisible pens, undercover devices are invaluable undercover aids—as long as they work and remain undiscovered.

Drops and Dead Drops

When an informer or agent leaves a message or secret information for the handler in a prearranged place, it is known as a dead letter drop. Simple, everyday signs, such as gum on a bench or a newspaper by a tree, are used to signal when a message has been left. This method means that the spy and handler do not have to risk meeting.

This apple looks innocent on the outside, but inside it hides a computer circuit.

A lump of rock fitted with a hidden transmitter sounds like a gimmick in a farfetched spy movie, but this device really existed. In 2006, in Moscow, Russia, men were seen walking back and forth near a lump of fake rock. The Federal Security Service of the Russian Federation (FSB) had taken an X-ray of the rock and it revealed a transmitter inside the rock. The men, walking past the rock were British agents, who were transmitting information. The FSB filmed these agents and, without them knowing, downloaded their intelligence.

Dead drop

THINK LIKE A TECHNICIAN

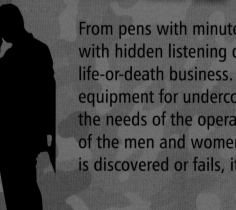

From pens with minute cameras to clothes buttons fitted with hidden listening devices, undercover equipment is a life-or-death business. The men and women who provide equipment for undercover officers and agents must balance the needs of the operation to get intel with the safety of the men and women on the ground. If the equipment is discovered or fails, it is game over for the agent.

Today's technological version of invisible ink is digital steganography. This method of hiding digital secret communication in images, recordings, or documents is very difficult to detect. Terrorists and criminals often use sophisticated online methods to hide their communications and carry out their crimes. Agencies try to keep one step ahead of them, but it is a challenge.

Hector Monsegur made his living as a hacker, getting into other people's online accounts and identities. In 2011, after Monsegur hacked a website connected to the FBI, a team of FBI agents arrived on his doorstep. Monsegur was offered the chance to work undercover for the FBI or face a lengthy jail sentence. He chose to work with the FBI.

This spy camera from 1955 is much larger than the microscopic ones used today.

As Monsegur communicated with other hackers, the FBI tracked all his online communications, which led them to other hackers and criminals. According to the FBI, the information from Monsegur's undercover work helped prevent more than 300 cyberattacks.

In the Dark, in the Distance

Thermal imaging creates pictures using infrared heat energy instead of light. It reveals the movements of people in the dark. Night vision goggles enable operatives to see in the dark. Spy satellites give crucial information about the whereabouts and activity of people being watched. The satellites travel around Earth, taking pictures of the ground below and transmitting the images to computers.

Before satellites, agents used carrier pigeons. During World War I, pigeons were fitted with a small camera. The birds flew over military sites to gain images of the enemy's weapons, then they would fly back to their handlers.

Carrier pigeon

ACT LIKE AN AGENT

Agents rely heavily on equipment to help them carry out missions. Here are just some of the items they use:
★ Watch (with a recording device)
★ Sunglasses (with a camera)
★ Gun

TAKE THE TEST!

Have you gotten a grip on undercover gadgets?

Surveillance is crucial in an undercover operation. Gadgets can reveal top-secret information. Have you been reading carefully?

Q1. Why were pigeons useful in World War I?

Q2. What method is used to take pictures in the dark?

Q3. What is digital steganography?

Q4. Why did Monsegur agree to work undercover for the FBI?

Q5. What happens in a dead letter drop?

Q6. Give one example of a sign that information has been delivered in a dead letter drop.

Q7. What was hidden inside a rock in Moscow and why?

Q8. Why is the dead letter drop used?

ANSWERS

Q1. They were fitted with small cameras to take pictures of enemy camps

Q2. Thermal imaging

Q3. A method of hiding digital secret communication in images, recordings, or documents

Q4. Because the FBI had discovered he was a hacker and he would have faced a long jail sentence if he had not agreed to work for them

Q5. An agent leaves information to be picked up by the handler in a prearranged place

Q6. Chewing gum on a bench or a newspaper by a tree

Q7. A transmitter by which information could be sent

Q8. So the spy and handler do not have to meet

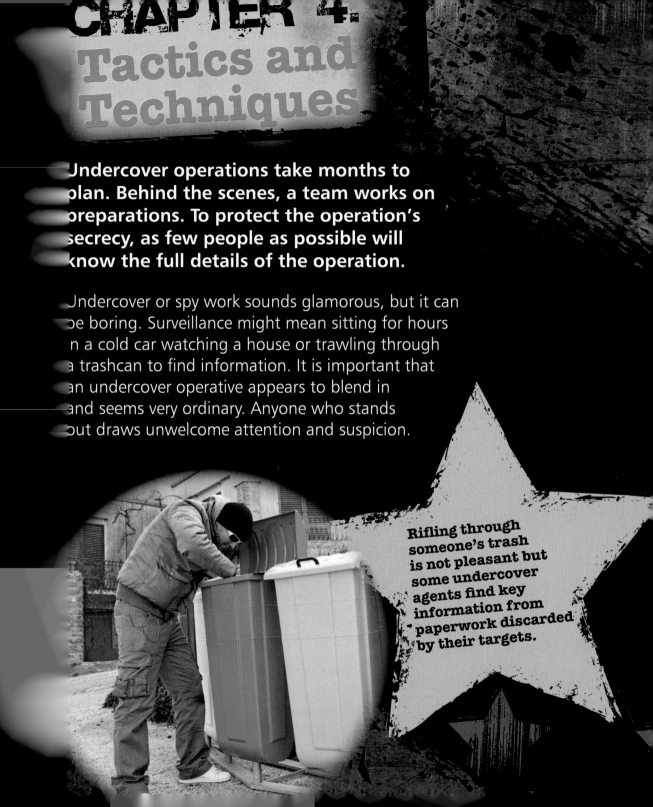

CHAPTER 4

Tactics and Techniques

Undercover operations take months to plan. Behind the scenes, a team works on preparations. To protect the operation's secrecy, as few people as possible will know the full details of the operation.

Undercover or spy work sounds glamorous, but it can be boring. Surveillance might mean sitting for hours in a cold car watching a house or trawling through a trashcan to find information. It is important that an undercover operative appears to blend in and seems very ordinary. Anyone who stands out draws unwelcome attention and suspicion.

Rifling through someone's trash is not pleasant but some undercover agents find key information from paperwork discarded by their targets.

Around the Clock

One operation took a year of around-the-clock surveillance on a suspected terrorist. When enough information was gathered, a team of 24 operatives from Delta, the US Army's Special Forces unit, and FBI agents snatched the wanted man outside his home. Not a single shot was fired. The success of the operation depended on secrecy and skill.

Building a legend

THINK LIKE A SPY

All agents use covers and legends. A cover is an alias with false details. A legend is a complex and detailed backstory, developed for long operations when an agent goes deep undercover, living a lie. The legend is a fictional personal and family history that is believable and memorable. If someone becomes suspicious and starts to make inquiries about the operative, agents make sure that there is a paper and online trail that backs up their legend.

Skills and Mental Aptitude

Undercover operations are not one-woman or one-man missions. A team of skilled experts helps set up any undercover operation and keep it secret. A case officer manages the operation and a handler is in charge of agents. Analysts make links between pieces of information, both facts and clues, to build up a picture of the situation.

Undercover agents are rigorously tested to make sure they are mentally and physically able to do the job. Any agent needs to be in peak physical condition. The FBI will not take anyone for their selection process unless they meet their rigorous physical standards.

The armed forces' elite units go through a grueling training to prepare them for the pressures of undercover operations.

To work as an FBI officer, recruits are tested in the following exercises, with only a 5-minute break in between each activity:

★ The number of sit-ups they can do in 1 minute
★ A timed 300-yard (300 m) sprint
★ The number of continuous push-ups they can do
★ A timed 1.5-mile (2.4 km) run

Undercover Skills

These are some key skills needed for undercover work:

★ Friendliness—an agent needs to work well with others. Someone who is argumentative or is unfriendly will not win over trust.
★ Problem-solving—an agent needs to think quickly
★ Observation skills—it is important to notice detail so an agent blends into the group they are trying to infiltrate
★ Adaptability—an agent or an informer needs to adapt to changing situations.

Undercover training

THINK LIKE A HANDLER

It is a difficult balance trying to recruit informers who will share foreign intelligence and run agents. The handler, also called a controller, must develop a strong relationship with the informer to make sure they feel protected and valued.

TAKE THE TEST!

How skilled are you?

You now know what kind of person can work undercover, but do you think you have the right skills? Test your powers of observation and recall with these questions:

Q1. What does a handler do?

Q2. What is another term for a handler?

Q3. Why does an agent need to be friendly?

Q4. Name one physical activity the FBI uses to check the fitness of recruits.

Q5. Why do agents need to blend in?

Q6. A legend needs to be memorized. What else does the legend need and why?

Q7. What is Delta?

Q8. Give one example of a surveillance activity.

ANSWERS

Q8. Watching a house from a car or going through trash

Q7. The US Army's Special Forces unit

Q6. A paper and online trail so it appears real if a suspicious person wants to check it is true

Q5. So they do not draw attention to themselves

Q4. Any of the following: sit-ups, push-ups, timed runs and sprints

Q3. To gain the trust of others

Q2. A controller

Q1. Looks after the agent or informer

CHAPTER 5:
Undercover Lives

Conflicts and wars are fought on the ground, at sea, and in the air by soldiers of opposing armies, firing weapons at each other. During a war, undercover operations and spies are often active in order to get information about the enemy's firepower and tactics.

Civil War Spies

During the American Civil War between the Confederates and Unionists, two women from opposite sides worked as spies. Maria Boyd, known as Belle, was born in 1844. The young woman shot and killed a drunken Union soldier who attacked her mother. From then on, Belle worked for the Confederates. She went to the Union camps, making friends with the soldiers, but all the time gathering information. On one occasion, after overhearing Union officers say they planned to destroy a town's bridges as they retreated, Belle braved a long journey to inform the Confederates about the impending Union tactics.

Maria Boyd

Harriet Tubman, born in 1822, escaped life as a slave. Although she was a wanted woman, Harriet returned to the South many times to lead her family and other slaves to freedom. During the Civil War, Tubman spied for the Unionists. She wandered unnoticed through rebel territory, collecting information that she passed to the Unionists. Armed with knowledge obtained by Tubman, the Unionists made several successful raids in coastal areas.

Harriet Tubman worked as a nurse as well as a spy.

THINK LIKE AN UNDERCOVER AGENT

Deep undercover, agents live a permanent lie. They stay with criminals who commit crimes. The agents must have great mental strength to hide their true feelings about the criminals while convincing them they are on their side.

No Ordinary Couple

There is no such thing as an ordinary person! The most ordinary-seeming people may hold very unusual secrets, and may be working as undercover operatives.

Richard and Cynthia Murphy lived an unremarkable life in a quiet area of New Jersey. They had two daughters who went to the local school. Richard stayed at home with the children, while Cynthia went to work. She had a well-paid job in New York City. One day in 2010, the road that the Murphys lived on was blocked with police cars—the FBI was raiding the Murphy's house.

Discoveries and Negotiations

It was discovered that the Murphy's names were false. The couple was in fact Vladimir and Lydia Guryev. They had been spying for Russia, obtaining information about the US government and its policies.

Some spies live unnoticed in their community, like the Murphys, until the arrival of the police turns their world upside down.

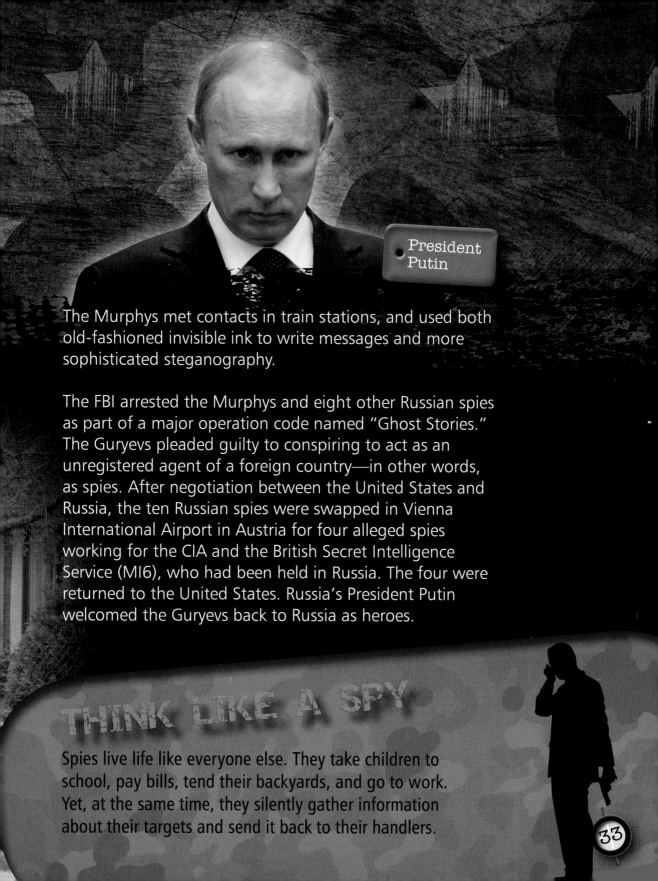

President Putin

The Murphys met contacts in train stations, and used both old-fashioned invisible ink to write messages and more sophisticated steganography.

The FBI arrested the Murphys and eight other Russian spies as part of a major operation code named "Ghost Stories." The Guryevs pleaded guilty to conspiring to act as an unregistered agent of a foreign country—in other words, as spies. After negotiation between the United States and Russia, the ten Russian spies were swapped in Vienna International Airport in Austria for four alleged spies working for the CIA and the British Secret Intelligence Service (MI6), who had been held in Russia. The four were returned to the United States. Russia's President Putin welcomed the Guryevs back to Russia as heroes.

THINK LIKE A SPY

Spies live life like everyone else. They take children to school, pay bills, tend their backyards, and go to work. Yet, at the same time, they silently gather information about their targets and send it back to their handlers.

Everyday People?

In some undercover operations, the agents do not need cover stories. They live and work openly in a particular field without aliases or legends. However, the agents are continually spying and sending critical information to their handlers.

The Cuban Case

Ana Montes was a well-respected and key member of the United States' Defense Intelligence Agency (DIA). She was a top analyst on Cuba. Little did her colleagues know that Montes had been recruited to spy for the Cubans. Montes disagreed with the US policy on this Caribbean country. The Cubans approached her, and she began working as a spy for them.

Ana Montes received special commendations for her work at the CIA. All the time, she was passing secret information to Cuba.

Montes had access to secret information. She worked hard during the day, and at home in the evening, she typed up everything she remembered. Then, she transferred the information onto special encrypted disks. After receiving instructions from the Cubans in code via short-wave radio, she would meet with her handler and hand over the disks.

A colleague became suspicious and Montes was interviewed. She took a polygraph (lie detector test) and passed. Four years later, there were reports of an undercover agent working in the United States for Cuba. The FBI looked at Montes' interview again and set up a surveillance operation. The FBI had a case against Montes but wanted to find her handler. However, they could not wait because Montes was about to gain access to information about the US attack on Afghanistan after the attacks of 9/11. They could not risk her passing on that information. Montes was arrested.

Surveillance operation

THINK LIKE AN UNDERCOVER AGENT

Unmasking a fellow spy takes time and patience. The person tracking a spy must take care to make sure the spy does not become suspicious and realize that their mission is compromised. The tracker must gather information and get evidence—all the time, building up a case to blow the spy's mission apart.

TAKE THE TEST!

Could you stay calm under pressure?

Can you hold your nerve under pressure? Staying calm is a key skill for an undercover operative—stay in control and test your knowledge:

Q1. What was "Ghost Stories?"

Q2. Why did Montes spy for the Cubans?

Q3. What is a polygraph?

Q4. Who were the Murphys?

Q5. Who were the Murphys spying for?

Q6. Why are spies used during wars?

Q7. Who was Tubman spying for?

Q8. Who was Boyd spying for?

ANSWERS

Q8. The Confederates
Q7. The Unionists
Q6. To find out about the enemy's firepower and tactics
Q5. Russia
Q4. The Guryevs
Q3. A lie detector test
Q2. Because she disagreed with US policy on Cuba
Q1. An operation in which 10 Russian spies were arrested

CHAPTER 6:
Spies Uncovered

Undercover operations are used to find out information that will help bring criminals to justice. They are also used to bring to a close complex and sensitive investigations, which rely on complete secrecy.

Operation Red Dawn to capture Iraqi leader Saddam Hussein came after an intense intelligence-gathering operation in the Tikrit area of Iraq over several months. United States forces gradually built up a picture of Saddam Hussein's likely whereabouts through tip-offs, interrogations of detainees, and rigorous analysis of information. Saddam was eventually found at the bottom of a hole and arrested.

Months of work led to the discovery of Saddam Hussein, hiding out in a "hole" covered by rocks and full of possessions.

Changing Sides

Anwar al-Awlaki

Morten Storm had a difficult life. By the age of 13, he was in trouble with the police. He then converted to Islam, but his views became extremist and dangerous. However, 10 years later, Storm questioned and then rejected these extreme beliefs. He contacted the Danish Intelligence services and began working for them as well as for the CIA.

According to Storm, the CIA tasked him to find suspected terrorist leader Anwar al-Awlaki, who was believed to be hiding out in the mountains in Yemen, and to pass on information about planned terrorist attacks. Anwar al-Awlaki was killed in a United States' air strike but the CIA denied that Storm's intel had led to the killing. Storm and the CIA argued, and Storm went public with his story. Neither the CIA nor the Danish Intelligence services have ever confirmed or denied Storm's account.

THINK LIKE A HANDLER

It is not easy living with the knowledge that an agent was imprisoned or killed because an operation went wrong. Handlers have to try to put aside their feelings if they were involved in a failed operation. They have to move on and focus on the next operation to make sure they keep those agents and informants as safe as possible.

Dangerous Careers

Undercover operations are dangerous. Agents are trained well. Handlers and officers support their informants. However, no one can ever truly predict how things will turn out.

The Spy Town

Rigorous training and preparation for operations can help agents deal with situations and unpredictable outcomes. Training takes place in locations specifically designed to help agents practice what they have been taught. Hogan's Alley is a town where no one lives. It is the FBI's training town where agents and FBI recruits put into practice the skills they have learned in training school. Armed forces special ops units such as the Green Berets and SEALs train and rehearse in realistic situations to prepare them for action.

Undercover operatives are always prepared to defend and protect their country.

Risks of the Job

In 2014, over a few weeks, demonstrators held antipolice protests in Oakland, California. Unknown to the protesters, plainclothes police officers had been mingling with them. Some demonstrators were suspicious and identified the two undercover officers. In fear of their lives, one of the officers turned his gun on the crowd.

In 1978, walking home one evening over a London bridge, in England, a man holding an umbrella brushed past the journalist Georgi Markov. Markov felt a jab on his leg but thought nothing of it. Three days later he was dead! A "bullet" in the spike of the umbrella had poisoned him. Police believe a Bulgarian agent killed him because of his political views. No one has ever been convicted of his death.

Stealth bomber

Working Together

Noshir Gowadia was an engineer at the defense company that built the B-2 stealth bomber. Gowadia sold highly classified information about technology used to make the bomber to several nations, including China. In a joint operation, the air force, US Customs, and other agencies built a case against him. In 2011, Gowadia was sentenced to 32 years in prison.

THINK LIKE A HANDLER

Informers are in a risky position and face threats from all sides. They face danger from the people they are informing on, and from the people to whom they are passing data. Handlers can threaten to blow informers' cover if they do not continue to provide the information needed.

Discovering Secrets

Working undercover takes commitment, bravery, and focus. The men and women who go undercover are asked to do so for the best interests of their community and country, to defend and protect against criminals and danger. Some people spy for political reasons. Others do it for money.

Web of Deceit

In the 1980s, Oleg Gordievsky worked in London, England, for the KGB. However, Gordievsky's political views changed, and he secretly began to work for MI6. At around the same time, a CIA agent working in Turkey, Aldrich Ames, changed his views about the United States' policies and began to work for the Soviet Union.

In 1987, President Reagan met with Oleg Gordievsky. After pressure from the president and British prime minister, Margaret Thatcher, Gordievsky was reunited with his family.

THINK LIKE A SECRET AGENT

In 1946, a group of schoolchildren from the Soviet Union presented the US Ambassador to the Soviet Union with a wooden copy of the Great Seal of the United States. US agents were suspicious (this was at a time when there was great mistrust between the Soviet Union and countries in the West). They checked the wooden seal for any hidden devices. Six years later, during which time the Seal had been hanging in the Ambassador's residence, a small device was finally found. The device had enabled the Russians to listen to conversations in the Ambassador's residence for the last six years without any intervention!

It is thought that information Ames had passed to the KGB led them to suspect Gordievsky of being a double agent. He was recalled to the Soviet Union and was placed under surveillance. However, during a morning jog, Gordievsky managed to send a message to his British handlers that he was under suspicion. The British successfully smuggled him out of the country in the trunk of a car. Meanwhile, US agents became suspicious of Ames' expensive cars and house, and he too was finally uncovered as a double agent.

Great Seal of the United States

Have You Got What It Takes?

If you want to work undercover, follow these steps and you may reach your career goal.

School

Study hard and graduate. Working undercover takes hard work and intelligence, not just physical strength. It helps if you are skilled in more than one language, especially if you want to be a handler.

Volunteer

Join clubs and groups that offer you the chance to improve your fitness and develop your team skills. Undercover work means being part of a team.

Be Flexible

If you decide the job is not for you and that your skills are best used in other areas of defense, you will still have gained valuable skills to use in another role.

Personality

Make sure your behavior and actions are always responsible. Agencies will check if you have a good character and are trustworthy. Stay out of trouble.

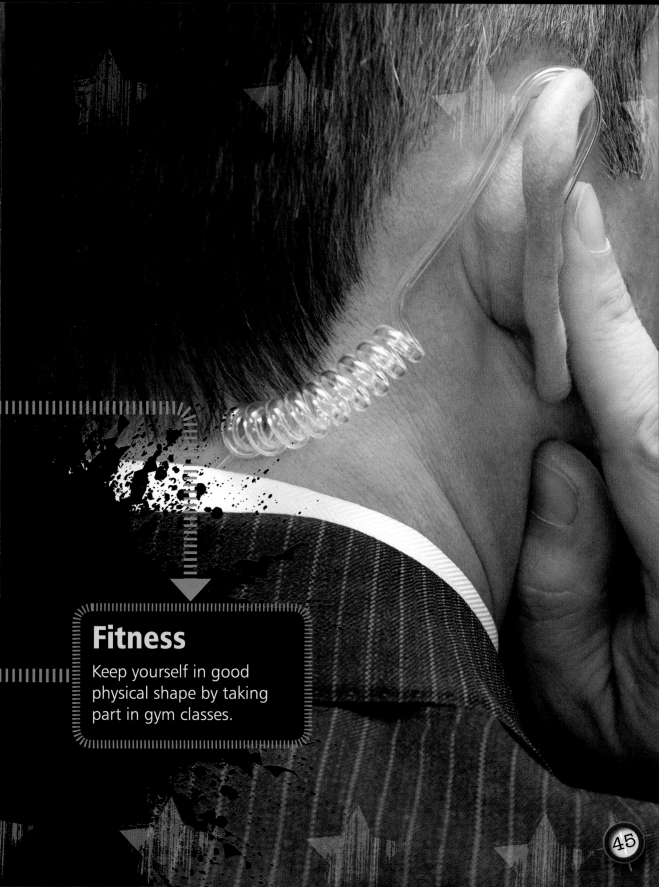

Fitness

Keep yourself in good physical shape by taking part in gym classes.

Glossary

alias false identity

armed forces the military including the army, navy, and air force

blown when an operation is exposed or an agent's identity is revealed

case officer someone who manages agents and runs operations

compound a large area that includes houses

confidential private

controller an officer in charge of agents (a handler)

counterfeit false

cover the pretend occupation of an agent or his or her reason for being somewhere

covert secret

double agent someone who says they are spying for their country but is spying for the enemy

elite special and exclusive

extremist someone with dangerously extreme views

hacker someone who breaks into secure websites

infiltrate to get into an organization in order to obtain information

informer someone who shares confidential information about an organization or activity

intel (short for intelligence), information about an enemy, its plans, and its power

legend a spy's made-up, detailed background

Mafia an organized criminal group working mainly in the United States, Italy, and Sicily

operation a mission

operative a person working on a mission

policy a course of action proposed by a government or individual

political to do with beliefs about the way a country is run

sensitive secret

smuggled brought into a country illegally

Special Forces elite units in the armed forces, often working on undercover operations

steganography a way of concealing secret messages or information within nonsecret text or data

For More Information

Books

Briggs, Andy. *How to be an International Spy: Your Training Manual, Should You Choose to Accept It.* Oakland, CA: Lonely Planet Kids, 2015.

Buller, Laura, Joe Fullman, and Ben Gilliland. *Top Secret: Shady Tales of Spies and Spying*. New York, NY: DK Publishing, 2011.

Gilbert, Adrian. *Spy School* (Spy Files). Richmond Hill, ON: Firefly Books, 2009.

Sutherland, Adam. *Undercover Operations* (On the Radar: Defend and Protect). Minneapolis, MN: Lerner Publishing Group, 2012.

Websites

Find out more about the FBI at:
www.fbi.gov/fun-games/kids/kids-about

You can take several online challenges to see if you have the skills to work in the British Secret Service at:
www.mi5.gov.uk

Learn more about the history of spies at:
www.spymuseum.org

Index